CW00925481

DOVER
PAST AND PRESENT

PAUL WELLS AND JEFF HOWE

The
History
Press

ACKNOWLEDGEMENTS

It has been an interesting journey for us both and although our main interest in Dover is usually centred around the castle and especially Western Heights, it is impossible to look at these hills and the people on them without letting one's interest get caught up in the rest of this truly fascinating town.

We have been spoilt with help from many people on our way and the most generous assistance has been given by Mr A. Studdal for contributing his wealth of knowledge of the Promenade Pier & Pavilion Co. to the project. Thanks also to Steve Brown for lending us his Jeep Wrangler to pose with Mik & Jane Gaffney's children, Taylor, Spencer and Finlay!

We are indebted to Ian Lilford for letting us use his train ferry photos; to Jennie Burgess for the use of her picture of Archcliffe Gate and her father, Smye-Rumsby, for the early photo of their premises in Snargate Street. Thanks also to Dover Harbour Board for the use of three photos, namely one of the Eastern Docks, Western Docks and one of Wellington Bridge; and to Dyer Architects for the use of their vision of the so-named iconic structure planned for the St James' redevelopment.

And last but not least of course, the wives! Our love and thanks to Sue and Jo for enduring lonely nights and weekends while their husbands were sat at desktop computers whilst drowning in a sea of books and papers.

First published 2009

The History Press
The Mill, Brimscombe Port
Stroud, Gloucestershire, GL5 2QG
www.thehistorypress.co.uk

© Paul Wells and Jeff Howe, 2009

The right of Paul Wells and Jeff Howe to be identified as the Authors
of this work has been asserted in accordance with the
Copyrights, Designs and Patents Act 1988.

ISBN 978 0 7524 5192 3

Typesetting and origination by The History Press
Printed in Great Britain

CONTENTS

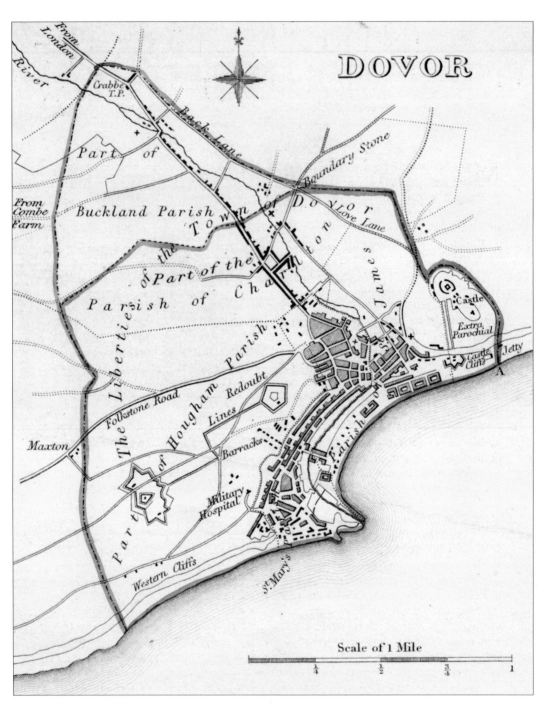

Dover, *c.* 1850.

INTRODUCTION

Many books have been written about Dover. Much has been said about the Iron Age fort that grew to become Dover Castle, the Bronze Age boat that is older than the pyramids, the *Classis Britannica* Roman fort and the 400-year-old Dover Harbour Board. That is not to mention the Crundalls, Mowlls, Adcocks and countless others that helped to make Dover into a nineteenth-century metropolis.

At its prime Dover housed a military garrison of around 8,000 men, was a Royal Navy Grand Fleet base and boasted five railway stations (including Shakespeare Halt). It is interesting to note that the Town Station was located in the long-since redeveloped Pier District, well away from the modern town with which we are familiar today.

The Pier District or just simply 'the Pier' as it was known, was home to Dover's first harbour and was the epicentre of mercantile Dover for several centuries. The area was congested with small cottages, latterly referred to as slums. These were cleared from the 1930s as the railway network expanded further. Nearly all of the street names have been lost. Indeed, there can't be many of us that can recall strolling down Round Tower Street, Water Lane, Middle Row or Strond Street. To wander across Blenheim Square today would be to dice with articulated trucks on the concreted enclosure there, adjacent to a mere memory of Beach Street.

Although Dover Castle has long dominated the skyline and the town's psyche, it is matched in enormity and outgunned in terms of artillery positions by the fortifications on the hill to the west of the town. The Western Heights defences came about when the British were fighting the American colonists during the late 1770s, and like the castle changed and grew to meet subsequent security threats along its way, resulting in one of the most protected hillsides in Europe – three main works, numerous artillery batteries and five miles of dry ditches, or moats.

Like the town, much has been demolished. In the town this was largely due to enemy shelling during the Second World War, together with what might be referred to as short-sighted or inappropriate planning decisions. Certainly Western Heights has had its fair share of planning faux pas; the demolition of the south entrance gate in 1963 to widen a road for a volume of traffic that never happened, the demolition and infilling of about a quarter of the moats and, believe it or not, a proposal in the 1960s to fill the moats with household refuse! At the time of writing, the Western Heights Preservation Society is working with English Heritage to improve access to the Drop Redoubt, the eastern-most fort on the hill. Unfortunately, most of that which remains is in an uncared for and derelict state (this excludes the Citadel which is in the care of the Home Office).

Along with its numerous railway stations, Dover once had more than its fair share of seaside piers too. Excluding the once-isolated Eastern Arm and South Pier which now form part of the Eastern Docks complex, Dover can still boast two piers today.

Prince of Wales Pier is still a pleasure pier, and one can still walk along and fish from the Admiralty Pier further westwards. The Promenade Pier & Pavilion Co. built a promenading pier in 1891 opposite the Burlington Hotel, across from Clarence Lawn (roughly where The Gateway is today). When the pier and pavilion were completed by 1901 it was possible to wander along the 900ft-long decking with one's lady-friend, and if wished, to be entertained in the pavilion by typical music hall acts such as Harold Montague's troupe, 'The Vagabonds', or to listen to Ghita Corri or Esme Atherden singing a ballad of the age or an excerpt from a Gilbert and Sullivan operetta.

The latter's was a real rags to riches story. Emma (Esme) Atherden was born in 'the Pier' in 1878 but by 1900 caused something of a sensation by becoming 'Dover's Royal College of Music Student', as the local papers had her. She even recorded on early phonograph cylinder for Thomas Edison's company before marrying Walter Hyde, an opera 'star' of the age who latterly became director of the British National Opera Company.

Perhaps it is reassuring to know that as well as Esme leaving some rare recordings, the Promenade Pier's main gates were sold off at auction when it was shut in 1927, and that these can be seen today guarding the entrance to a farm in the depths of the west Kent countryside – if you can find them!

1

DOVER GARRISON

This late Victorian view of Dover Castle nicely represents the military town and environs. We see this iconic structure and we know we're in Dover. What we may not know is that there is another fortress on the western hill opposite the castle, and lesser known still is the Victorian fort or so-called 'Palmerston's Folly' located behind the photographer of the above image, namely Fort Burgoyne.

St Mary in Castro in around 1860 and today. It is supposed that the mound on which the Pharos or Roman lighthouse sits dates back to the Iron Age and is at the heart of the much later Norman castle. It dates to the first century AD and is one of a pair, the remains of the other being within the Drop Redoubt fort on the Western Heights. The principal being that incoming shipping would navigate between the two to safely enter the Roman quay. The Pharos is

12.5 metres tall with a fifteenth-century octagonal belfry 3.3 metres high.

St Mary in Castro is a Saxon church which fell into disrepair and was latterly used as a coal store. In 1862 restoration work took place, and in 1888 it was finished with the tower being completed.

Dover Castle in around 1895 and a similar view in 2005. Today's Lord Warden of the Cinque Ports is the Admiral Lord Michael Boyce, whose inauguration was carried out at Dover Castle in April 2005 with the full pomp and circumstance that has always accompanied this most prestigious of occasions. The first image is believed to date from 1895, when Robert Gascoyne-Cecil, 3rd Marquess of Salisbury, was installed as Lord Warden. The buildings on the right, the old married quarters, date from around 1850 and were demolished along with many other mid-Victorian accommodation blocks in the castle during the 1960s and 1970s. The area is now known as Palace Green after the adjacent Palace Gate, and this is where historical re-enactments and other events for the public are now carried out.

Peverell's Tower in around 1920 and today. Following the Norman Conquest, William de Peverell, Constable of Dover Castle, lent his name to this well-known landmark.

When built, the walls of the tower and adjacent curtain wall would have been much higher than today. The heights of many of the walls and towers had been reduced during the eighteenth century to allow greater effectiveness of the modern artillery then mounted.

The cottage was originally the Sergeant-Major's house and dates from the late eighteenth century, and was the castle Head Custodian's dwelling until the early 1990s. Both the cottage and tower have recently been conserved and modernised with a view to hiring them out as holiday homes to paying guests, a service which has proved to be very popular.

Grand Shaft Barracks in about 1930 and today. These barracks were mostly demolished in 1964, some 160 years after being built. They were originally known as Western Heights Barracks and were constructed for around 800 officers and men. They became known as Grand Shaft Barracks once the triple spiral staircase of the same name had been constructed. The two large blocks in the foreground are soldiers barracks, ranges A & B and to the right, the top of the shaft itself.

The last building to go from this site was the troop stable block which was only knocked down in 1997 due to its ruinous state. Over the last forty years there have been many attempts to redevelop the site into a hotel complex. Fortunately these have been turned down by the district planners and the site is now a local nature reserve.

Garrison Chapel in 1906. The Garrison Chapel dates from around 1859, a time when there was major change on the Western Heights. Much building work was being carried out and the defences therein strengthened to resist a largely imagined attack from France. This fear was due to several factors, including the launch of the French ironclad warship, *Le Gloire* (The Glory), the advent of rifled artillery and Emperor Napoleon III coming to power.

Adjacent to the chapel were other military buildings including an infants' school, coal yard, and Royal Engineers Office. All were demolished in the early 1960s to make way for a housing programme for the staff working in the Citadel, then a prison. As you can see, there is no evidence at all of any of the Victorian structures on this site.

Royal Military Hospital in about 1918 and today. The military hospital on Western Heights was built around 1803, and was one of the earliest permanent structures built on the Heights. The only other permanent buildings constructed around this time would have been Grand Shaft Barracks, the Drop Redoubt Fort (phase one, less its caponniers) and elements of the Citadel. The military hospital is often not considered when speaking of Western Heights as it is more associated with the area known more commonly as Archcliffe.The brick tower at the top of the photograph is Archcliffe Gate (see p. 16).

During the Second World War the building was used as the regional headquarters for the Royal Engineers. The building was demolished in around 1962 along with others at Archcliffe Yard as part of a scheme to bring light industry to Dover. This period saw the Racole Ladder and Parker Pen factories built in their place.

The road now known as Channel View Road was originally Hospital Road and the hospital plot is now occupied by Burgess Engineering Group offices.

Western Heights in about 1910 and today. This is looking up the Barrier Ditch, one of the many dry moats or ditches on the Western Heights. There were once about five miles of ditches here, but sadly much was destroyed in the 1960s. The Barrier Ditch was one of three ditches that ran from the defences to the cliff edge and formed a physical barrier to any invading force coming from the south-west of Dover. This is a training exercise by Kent Royal Engineers 'A Company', who are spanning the ditch, which is about 40ft wide and 30ft deep.

Most of this ditch has now disappeared following the extension and widening of the A20 in the early 1990s. The other obvious feature on these pictures is the Victorian Officers' Mess (centre top), which is still used today as part of the immigration removal centre.

Grand Shaft in 1909 and today. The current Grand Shaft Guardroom on Snargate Street is a replica of the original Georgian building which was demolished in the 1960s. It was built in 1995 by the IMPACT group. The original was of course a guardroom for the triple spiral staircase connecting the street to the barracks above. To the right of the guardroom is the Wesleyan chapel built in 1834 and, again, knocked down in the 1960s as the congregation migrated to the new Methodist church in the High Street. At the rear of the chapel are vaults, still extant, containing the remains of some well-known Dover families, including the Killicks.

The chapel site is now part of the National Car Rental premises and is now just a car park.

The sign in front of the chapel beside the bustled ladies advertises a Wesleyan minister coming from London to preach and nicely dates this photograph to 1909.

Archcliffe Gate in about 1932 and today. The south entrance to the Western Heights Garrison, Archcliffe Gate was built during the Victorian phase, around 1860. During the second half of the nineteenth century, much was done to enlarge the defences, including major building projects at the Drop Redoubt and new barracks, gun batteries and ditches all around the Heights. Fort Burgoyne behind Dover Castle was also built in this period. Dover must have been a busy place then. The Archcliffe Gate was protected by a ditch or moat built at a right-angle to it and stretching from right in front towards the cliff edge, terminating above Limekiln Street. The ditch was protected with gunrooms and rifle galleries and, of course, a retractable bridge.

This early picture shows Sergeant Sidney John Dudley Burgess of the 1st Battalion of the Royal Sussex Regiment, standing outside the gate wearing 'civvies'.

During the 1960s about twenty acres of War Department land was bought up by the Dover Corporation (later to become the Ministry of Defence and Dover District Council respectively) for redevelopment. The idea was to convert the land to light industrial use and create jobs. Anticipating a big take-up of the scheme, the Archcliffe Gate was demolished in 1963 to widen the road. The rubble was bulldozed into the adjacent ditch and smoothed over. Some parts remain but are difficult to interpret.

There were only ever two motor repair workshops on the Heights using old War Office (MOD) buildings and land as a result of this scheme.

Grand Shaft Barracks *c.* 1900 and today. The barracks on the cliff top are Grand Shaft Barracks. They were known as Western Heights Barracks up to the completion of the Grand Shaft in 1807. The triple spiral staircase was built between the cliff top and Snargate Street to move the maximum number of troops from the barracks to the seafront in the shortest possible time in case of invasion by the French. The site comprised soldiers' barracks, officers' quarters as well as a gymnasium, stables, gun shops, tailor shops, kitchens and all the necessary services needed to keep an army running.

Unfortunately most of the barracks were pulled down in 1964. The location was used in the 1965 film *The War Game* by Peter Watkin, which was about life during a nuclear war. The semi-demolished barracks looked like blocks of flats that had taken the brunt of an atomic bomb blast.

2

WESTERN DOCKS

The Harbour, Dover.

There are several known photographs similar to the above view, most of them entitled 'The Viaduct'. However they show us so much more than the now familiar road bridge over the docks. This was the area where Dover's commercial harbour started over 500 years ago, and although there isn't much left of value to see (with a few notable exceptions), Dover's established trade links with the Continent were born here. And now of course we have viaducts at both ends of Dover front!

Admiralty Pier, 18 January 1881 and today. This was the day of the big storm in Dover, and this date stuck in people's minds for some years afterwards. In fact it was Dover's biggest storm for forty-four years. Around the town, houses lost their roofs, cellars were flooded and in the harbour vessels were completely submerged. Even the Admiralty Pier didn't escape. Huge 1.5 ton blocks were ripped up from their seatings and iron gates ripped from their hinges. The mail train was disrupted due to the rails being torn up and lampposts were snapped off. Iron railings were ripped away and telegraph wires destroyed. The damage done was estimated to be £10,000 – around £5 million based on today's average wage.

Dover Harbour about 1880 and 2008. Believe it or not there are over 125 years between these two images. The *Calais-Douvres* started carrying passengers across the Channel in 1878 along with her sister ships, *Bessemer* and *Castalia*. Each ship could carry about 1,000 passengers, but the ships were not particularly fast or manoeuvrable and were withdrawn from service.

The Speedferries *Speed One* started speeding between the English and French coasts in 2004 from the Eastern Docks, moving to the Western Docks in 2007. Unfortunately the company went bankrupt in 2008.

This view will be transformed as soon as the Western Docks undergoes further planned enlargement over the next few years.

Commercial Quay *c.* 1923 and today. These rail tracks lead the eye into Union Quay and Commercial Quay. The modern A20 dual carriageway runs along this site now, but when this early picture was taken this stretch of road ran from Strond Street in the Pier District into Commercial Quay or turned right towards Wellington Bridge.

If you were stood where the photographer was to take the above picture ninety years ago, you would be able to walk along Commercial Quay and buy a pint in nearly each property on the left! There are nine pubs as far as the eye can see. These included the Golden Anchor Hotel, Wellesley Inn, Alexandra Dining Rooms, New Commercial Quay Inn and the Barley Mow Inn to name a few. What a great shame that these old properties have been swept away.

The 2009 picture shows the area transformed. Strond Street is no more. Along with Customs House Quay it's now just a memory, the area having been given over to a no-go area within the Western Docks truck park and a private boatyard. There are remnants of Strond Street within the Western Docks, but these are limited to kerb stones, drain covers and cats' eyes which show where the road once was.

Outer Harbour *c.* 1890 and today. This charming steamboat was photographed in the outer harbour, with its polished brass funnel, fluttering pennants and smart skipper pictured against a once familiar view. Long gone are Lukey's vaults, the Customs House, Bradley Brothers' Grain Warehouse, not forgetting the buildings on Western Heights: the Royal Military Hospital, South Front Barracks and the cliff-top married quarters which are visible here.

All of the waters in this image are due to be land-filled when enlargement of the Western Docks starts sometime soon. The Hoverport has already being demolished in preparation for the works ahead.

Blenheim Square
c. 1860 and today.
Dover Sailors' Home
stood at Blenheim
Square which was in
the heart of the Pier
District when built in
1855. Kelly's *Directory
of Kent 1862* states
the following about
the Home:

The Sailors' Home
and refuge for
shipwrecked sailors
of every nation, a
commodious and
handsome edifice,
was erected in
Blenheim Square
in 1855. It is open to the public for inspection daily (except Sundays) from 1 a.m. to 6 p.m.
Connected with the Home is a free reading room and library of 2,000 volumes, sixty-five of which
were contributed by HM Queen. It is an institution well worthy of support and subscriptions will
be thankfully received by the Treasurer, the Revd W. Yate. There is accommodation in the home
for forty persons and since the opening, upward of 150 wrecked crews of various nations, forty
of which were French, have found refuge there. In front of the home is a Russian mortar taken at
Hango and presented to the home by Captain Hall and the officers and crew of HM ship, *Blenheim*.

Reverend Yate was connected with the church of St John Mariner which was also in the
Pier District, being in Middle Row, just off Blenheim Square. He founded the Dover Sailors'
Home, and served as minister at the church for thirty-one years. Reverend Yate died in 1877; his

memorial tablet was
on the wall of the
church. I wonder if it
got demolished with
the buildings or was
saved?

Unfortunately the
whole area is now the
Dover Freight Clearance
Centre. The rows of
two-up, two-down
terraced houses,
churches and other
Victorian buildings are
long demolished.

Customs House Quay in the late 1940s and today. John Lukey & Sons' vault, latterly the Continental Express Ltd bonded store was demolished in 1950 along with the Pavilion Bars building. Here they are seen against the backdrop of the Citadel and the Harbour Station with Strond Street running past their rear. The gap between Fremlins Hostelry and Coast Line Seaways looks like bomb damage from the Second World War. The North London Demolition & Excavation Company carried out the demolition work of the buildings shwon above, and was also responsible for the eventual loss of the Esplanade and Burlington hotels. Today the site is part of the Pier District truck park.

Wellington Dock *c.* 1930 and today. *TS* (Turbine Steamer) *Canterbury (II)* was launched in December 1928 for Southern Railways as a passenger vessel. However with the outbreak of war a decade later in September 1939 she was to take on a much more important role. Not only did she see service during Operation Dynamo, the evacuation of Dunkirk, but she was also used during the Normandy landings in 1944. She returned to Southern Railways service in July 1945 and was finally scrapped in 1964 after a very distinguished history.

Although the *TS Canterbury (II)* is long gone, Wellington Dock remains largely unchanged, at least for the moment. Dover Harbour Board plans to redesign the Western Docks and this work will involve moving Dover Marina, currently based at the dock to a new marina near to Prince of Wales Pier. This scheme is to allow berthing for at least four ferries this side of the harbour.

Let's hope that Fairbairn Engineering's crane built in 1868 and evident in both pictures (far right) will stay.

Harbour Station *c.* 1910 and today. The Harbour Station dates to 1861 and in its
original form included the Station Master's Office and a first class waiting room.
A large canopy covered the platforms on both sides, including the removable section
of platform on the 'down' side of the station which could be wheeled out of the way
to provide access to the promenade railway junction. This station closed in 1927
and this was when the various windows were bricked up and it was converted into
a bonded warehouse. Today it is a P&O training centre and is a Grade Two listed
building, and the platforms are long gone.

The old picture shows a remarkable array of adverts, including those for Globe
Polish, Roses Lime Juice and The Standard.

Western Docks train ferry berth in the 1980s and today. Right in the middle of the old picture, taken from the back of the ferry, you can see the Harbour Station's truncated tower, to the left of that Channel House, (P&O Ferries headquarters) and to the right the old customs clearance house. This scene hasn't changed all that much, with the obvious exception of there are now no railway lines. The Southern Railway built the train ferry dock here in 1933 and it opened three years later, the first ferry to use it being the *Hampton Ferry*, one of three new ships built by the railway company. The other two were famously *Twickenham* and *Shepperton*.

The dock consisted of a gate which was raised up from the floor of the dock and water would be pumped out of the enclosure when a ferry had docked. This would correct the water level in the dock in order that the loading ramp was level so that freight could be safely loaded.

The early picture is taken from one of the ferries looking out to the railway sidings. This dock closed in 1988. Today the area is a freight clearance centre for articulated lorries. These go from the Eastern Docks and curiously still use one of the old train ferries, *Nord Pas de Calais* which works as a conventional ro-ro ferry from that side of the harbour.

Train ferry dock in the 1980s and today. Here we see the 1936 train ferry dock again, but this time with the *Saint-Germain* docked for loading. She commenced train ferry services from Dover to Dunkerque in 1951 and as well as operating from the train ferry berth operated from the Eastern Docks. She was repainted in the familiar Sealink colours in 1969. Her history involves several collisions, including one in 1979 with a freighter off Calais,  killing two people, injuring four and causing herself considerable damage.

In the later picture we can see the ferry dock gate in its upright position and the aggregate processing terminal for marine-dredged material run by Brett Hall Aggregates which now occupies this area. In 1988 the *Saint-Germain* was broken up for scrap in India.

'The Viaduct' on 7 May 1932 and today. This impressive column of troops marching over the Pier District viaduct past Elvey's mineral water factory was assembled to greet the visit of the official mission from the government of Hejaz and Nejd headed by Emir Fiesal. Ibn Saud brought together several territories in 1932 to constitute

Saudi Arabia, which must have happened very soon after the date of this photo.

As the French steamer *Empress* arrived flying her flag at half mast (the French President Paul Doumer had been assassinated the day before and had died on 7 May), a twenty-one gun salute was fired from Dover Castle.

The soldiers are the 1st Battalion Seaforth Highlanders. The Emir and his entourage were greeted by the Mayor and Town Council, and Emir Fiesal inspected the troops before boarding the train for London.

Pier District *c.* 1920 and today. This view looking down towards the Admiralty Pier from South Military Road shows much activity. On the horizon we can see the completed breakwater and Admiralty Pier with a row of block ships in the West Harbour mouth. The Marine Station was completed by 1914 and adjacent to it is the now-demolished Town Station with Beach Street to its rear and, of course, Lord Warden House to its east.

The National Sailors Home is still there, as is Middle Row. To the right of the old viaduct is the Archcliffe Yard, a Royal Army Service Corps establishment, together with Archcliffe Fort still showing its two-storey gatehouse and south-eastern defences prior to them being demolished to create extra space for the growing railway. Immediately opposite the entrance to the Fort is a nice row of now-vintage trucks.

The only structures still present are few and far between. Slum clearance and redevelopment account for most of the present view. The old Pier District is now primarily a concreted truck park.

Today, Archcliffe Fort is at last being used. It is inhabited by the St Martin's Emmaus Trust, a centre for homeless people where they '... offer homeless people a home, work and the chance to rebuild their lives in a supportive environment. There are currently nineteen communities around the UK and several more in development.'

X marks where Grandad worked (Good ole' Days)

Strond Street in the 1920s and today. Strond Street is another of those Pier District streets to have long disappeared under a mire of clearance and redevelopment. The name Strond comes from 'strand' which originally meant shallow shore or river edge. I'm sure most of us know of a Strond, or Strand, Street or Road where we live or in a nearby town. Strond Street was in the epicentre of Dover's first commercial harbour and its Holy Trinity Church was a beautiful example of the gothic revival movement, built in 1833 during the reign of William IV. Unfortunately it was demolished in 1945.

The *Evellyn Marion* was a 757 ton German cargo ship, probably built in 1909 as the *Stephanie*. She was broken up in 1939.

Admiralty Pier *c.* 1920 and today. To the left of the image can be seen the Dover Turret which was opened in 1881 as part of Dover's coast defence capability. It comprised a pair of 16in, 81 ton muzzle-loading guns. The two guns could rotate through 360 degrees on steel rollers, achieved by a steam engine operating in the bowels of the structure. The whole assembly weighs about 900 tons, and amazingly the guns are still there inside the turret. Although access to the Dover Harbour Board Admiralty Pier is open, access to the sadly derelict turret is not. The locomotive in this picture is the *Sir Geraint*, a King Arthur class built in 1925. She ran mainline services until withdrawn in 1958. By 1968 all steam traction had been withdrawn in Great Britain.

Wellington Bridge *c.* 1930 and today. His Grace the Duke of Wellington, Lord Warden of the Cinque Ports was the first person to officially cross the bridge bearing his name. Wellington Bridge was officially opened on 13 November 1846 by the Duke and he crossed it by horse-drawn carriage after declining to walk across it. He was seventy-eight years of age then. He had been consulted throughout the bridge's design and creation, and crossed it to a salute of guns by one of the Western Heights batteries. A guard of honour was also present in the form of the 43rd Light Infantry.

The bridge was intended to join the tidal outer harbour and Wellington Dock, the original Pent. The project was very lavish and included demolishing many properties along Union Quay and removing thousands of wagon loads of spoil.

Marine Station *c.* 1930 and today. Dover Cruise Terminal One as it is now known, was built prior to the First World War and was used for military rail movements until it reopened after the war in 1918 as the South Eastern & Chatham Railway terminus.

This area of Dover was the centre of rail activities for many years, indeed the famous *Golden Arrow* service would arrive and depart from this railway station until it ceased operation in the 1980s.

The ornate memorial was unveiled on 28 October 1922 by Mr H. Cosmo Bonsor, Chairman of the South Eastern & Chatham Railway. Inscribed into the stone are the names of 5,222 SECR rail workers who served in the First World War, of which 556 lost their lives in the conflict.

Rail activities finished for good at the station in 1994 and the building remained in a derelict state until conversion to a cruise terminal.

Old Town railway yard around 1990 and today. The area down by the Admiralty Pier was once a major railway depot which connected Dover's five railway stations, and was responsible for taking freight in and out of the country via the train ferries. Charlie Howe is seen standing at the old train ferry marshalling yard next to one of the service's diesel shunting locomotives, number 08 908. Charlie joined the Southern Railway in February 1946 at the age of fifteen as a cleaner boy cleaning the steam locomotives, and worked his way up to become a main line engine driver in 1966. During his career on the railway he drove many mainline locomotives including the famous *Golden Arrow* train. He retired three weeks shy of fifty years' service in 1996.

This area is now a lorry park and little of the railway infrastructure survives here. The railway still carries passengers from Dover Priory station to Charing Cross via the Shakespeare Cliff tunnel, but completely bypasses this once busy part of the town.

Now and again the subject of reinstating the boat train resurfaces...

Harbour Station in the early twentieth century and today. What a pity the canopy and footbridge have disappeared. In the old photograph we can see both platforms – the left one being retractable to provide access to the promenade railway. The platforms and roof were removed around 1929.

The modern view shows a station building as a shadow of its former self. The sidings are long gone and the area a truck park. Has the romance gone out of train travel?

3

EASTERN DOCKS

Along with Dover Castle, the
White Cliffs are synonymous with
the town. They have become a
brand image for Dover much like
the Sydney Opera House has for
Australia, or the Eiffel Tower has
for France. They have been made
famous in literature, song and
prose and during the Second World
War the sight of the White Cliffs
symbolised home for returning
British servicemen. And home
meant safety and family.

Of course we can't walk along
underneath them very far now
because of the huge port terminal
which has grown up at their base
over the last 100 years or so. To
see the White Cliffs of Dover we
have to get on a ferry or walk to
Admiralty Pier at the Western
Docks.

The Eastern Docks have
reached full capacity and in the
next few years we will see major
reconstruction of the Western
Docks.

Eastern Docks around 1920, in 1969 and today. We all know Dover Eastern Docks. Even those that only come to Dover to get to France are familiar with today's sprawling dock. To call it just a ferry terminal seems rather inadequate considering the huge expanse it covers today.

The first of these pictures shows the overhead ropeway which opened in 1930 and brought coal from Tilmanstone Colliery to the docks as fuel. In this picture we can also see the GPO building (centre), to its right the site of the new car ferry jetties to be opened in 1953 next to the South Pier, and to its left the old oil storage tanks.

In the second picture things have changed quite a bit. There is a lot of land reclamation at the far end (the Camber) and the aerial ropeway has gone. Coal was out and new oil tanks were in. The 1953 car ferry berth is in full operation and adjacent to it we can see more land reclamation. The Hoverport is there too but off the page. The building bottom right is the 1953 reception building which housed a restaurant and shop, etc., and this can also be seen in the 2009 photo, centre right with the curved foyer.

Many of those that walk the cliffs above wonder at the metal fence-like framework that runs along this stretch of the cliff. Why did the cliffs need a fence here? There are no hints at the answer looking down on today's harbour, but these oil tanks hold the key. The cliff-edge fence was to stop chalk and other debris falling down and plunging into the tanks. Now you know!

This image of the Camber was taken during the First World War. The Camber was formed by the building of the Eastern Arm in 1901 and the South Pier adjacent to it. This area has seen much development during the last 100 years, but in 1918 this was a haven for motor launches. Dover's first International Hoverport was constructed nearby in 1967, the landfill being partly formed by the depositing of about 45,000 tons of spoil from Western Heights. Having said this, it is often overlooked that the very first hovercraft service worked from here in 1966 under the auspices of Townsend Hover Service.

Today this area has been infilled as the dock has grown ever larger.

DOVER ADMIRALTY HARBOUR—EASTERN ARM.
Commenced January, 1901.
Finished December, 1904.
Length 3320 feet.

Eastern Arm in 1905 and today.
The Eastern Arm was started in 1901
and completed in 1904. It is 3,320ft
long and was part of a massive building
programme to create a harbour at
East Cliff. Although Dover's original
harbour was on the western side of the
town, this soon reached capacity, just as
the Eastern Docks has today. The Western
Docks are soon to be enlarged.

When this early photo was taken
the breakwater wasn't yet completed.
The breakwater was completed by 1908
and is about 4,000ft long.

East Cliff before 1891 and today. Quite a bit of the East Cliff has been blasted away since this pre-1891 photograph was taken. This was done at the turn of the century when the harbour was first being developed. We know it's pre-1891 as there are no Promenade Pier workings. Castle Jetty juts out into the bay, and is so much more obvious than now, over 100 years later. A new dock exit road opened in 2009, and continuing in a stream of constant dock enlargement, even more of this jetty is now covered by land reclamation.

The cliffs are really clear in the old picture and it's possible to make out the scarp of East-Demi Bastion (top right), one of the castle's outer defences. The valley where the modern A2 runs onto the Jubilee Way viaduct can be seen too. Today most of the land to the east of the castle is covered with trees. This is a result of neglect and most are self-sown sycamores.

Castle Jetty about 1890 and 2008. The jetty was built to stop the eastward drift of shingle along the coast which had previously caused the erosion of Dover's sheltered harbour then at the Western Docks, and which also caused shipping channels to become blocked. Work began in 1752 and was completed by two years later.

This early picture shows the jetty with timber decking which was fitted sometime in the late nineteenth century. Following an archaeological review of the jetty in 2005, a new road has been built which it is hoped will ease freight traffic congestion leaving the Eastern Docks. Unfortunately another portion of Castle Jetty has been lost under this road.

A large section of it is already under the road, the inner end having started directly under the east cliff when the adjacent area was just a beach.

4

TOWN

22365 Dover. Market Square,

I suppose we all consider the Market Square to be the centre of the town. But in this section we will take a wander as far as Charlton Green, the church, the Burlington Hotel, St James, Snargate and Folkestone Road. And of course to Binfields wine merchants.

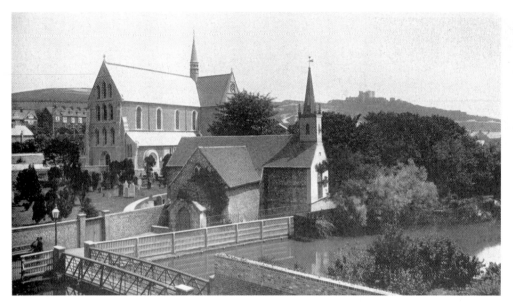

Charlton Church in about 1895 and today. Today's modern church of St Peter and St Paul dates back to 1891. It was finished in 1893 and is adjacent to old St Peter's which had become too small for its congregation. The original church is first mentioned in documents from the mid-twelfth century. Unusually there is no documented evidence for its existence between then and 1827 when it was rebuilt to increase its size.

It is unknown whether any of the earliest church existed in the rebuilt version. It was subsequently demolished anyway in 1895. The church we have today suffered during the Second World War having been hit by two shells on two separate occasions. As a result it suffered structural damage and lost its east windows. Repairs, including new windows, were carried out in 1952.

Dover sorting office in 1959 and 2008. This lot look like they're about to get down to some serious eating! It's a British Railways Southern Region, Dover Motive Power Depot dinner. In other words, they're all BR employees (and wives and girlfriends) from the Dover Rail Depot established in the Pier District. When this was taken, steam locomotives were still being used alongside diesel and electric so there would have been a large cross-section of talents in this room. Charlie Howe (see page 36) is there with his wife Iris on the end of the middle table on the right-hand side of the photo.

When this picture was taken the hall belonged to the Dover & District Co-operative Society but ended up being part of the Royal Mail sorting office. The modern picture shows it about to be demolished to be redeveloped as flats... it's gone completely now.

Connaught Park in about 1895 and today. The thirty-acre Connaught Park was opened by the Duke and Duchess of Connaught on 14 July 1884. It was laid out on former farmland below Dover Castle at a cost of £2,700. The new park featured meandering paths, an ornamental fountain with a lake and a drinking fountain donated by Alderman Astley. The once magnificent whale bone arch was removed for good in 1966 due to continued vandalism.

A commemorative Holm oak was planted to mark the opening of the park and this has flourished into the enormous tree that can still be seen today. It was joined by two more planted by St Mary's CE Primary School and the Dover Society in 1983 and 2008 respectively.

Our Lady Chapel in 1961 and today. Customers of Smye-Rumsby, the marine electronics company on Snargate Street, must be blessed when they enter the premises as it opened for business in March 1906 as Our Lady of Pity and St Martin Chapel with a seating capacity of 250 to 300. It was a replacement for an earlier chapel that stood in the Elizabeth Street area of the Pier District.

Indeed the words *Deo* and *sub invocations beatae Mariae et sancti Martini* are still there hidden behind the modern signage on the front of the building. We are lucky that this building, which has many original features still present, survived the war years when so much was lost in this area, including the famous Hippodrome theatre.

Having survived the First World War, the chapel became redundant by the second and was sold for £1,304. Purchased by Smye-Rumsby, the building was a replacement for their smaller stores in town. A second floor was installed, and inside the apse the parquet flooring still remains as a reminder of the former use.

If you ever have cause to go in or pass by, look up and you'll be able to see a cross set into the masonry above the front door.

Snargate Street as seen here in the 1920s can be considered as the once High Street of Dover's Pier District. Prior to the Second World War it was a busy street scene bustling with shoppers, tradesmen, soldiers and sailors. This was an area with more than its fair share of churches, pubs and hotels and at one point the Grand Shaft provided a route for soldiers housed in the cliff-top barracks on Western Heights access to the nocturnal delights of this once-busy street.

Stretching to the horizon, this early picture shows us Old Post Office, Prince Arthur and the Victory pubs. Also there is Forrester greengrocers, Hearn potato agent, the Ordance and York House Inn.

Camden Crescent in the late 1800s and today. Camden Crescent must have looked pretty impressive as a row of ten four-storey houses when built in 1840. Only four of the houses remain due to enemy action during the Second World War. Charles Dickens stayed in one of the houses when he was writing *Bleak House* in 1852.

Now mostly flats, at the time of writing one of the top floor two-bedroom flats is for sale at around £120,000 leasehold.

The Roundhouse from a 1931 auction catalogue and today. Shipdem House was built by John Shipdem, the Town Clerk and Register of Dover Harbour, in 1791. It was later referred to as the Round House, for obvious reasons. It is reputed that the ends and sides were circular in order that the Devil couldn't catch the owner in a corner!

This unique house boasted a library, smoking room, reading room, two bars, billiard rooms and had a 98ft long frontage onto Townwall Street.

It is under the current Townwall Street that its remains lie, having been demolished following severe damage during the Second World War.

Woolcomber Street in about 1897 and proposed view for 2012. The inaugural opening of the Hotel Burlington was on Saturday 24 July 1897 and was celebrated by a music luncheon featuring the bands of The Seaforth Highlanders, the 2nd Battalion East Surrey Regiment, the Dover Corporation Band and the Dover Bay Glee Singers! Only the wealthy and influential of Dover were invited.

However this was not the building's first incarnation. It was built in the 1860s as the Clarenden Hotel, soon to be renamed the Imperial. The building was eventually split into flats, being renamed Burlington Mansions. It was demolished after the Second World War having suffered significant damage by enemy action. If the Burlington was still here today, it would be on the petrol filling station site on Townwall Street and reach across to the Gateway flats.

The proposed replacement is a product of Dover Pride; 'a partnership of business, local and regional organisations and the people of Dover. Our aim is to make the town a great place to live, work and visit. The partnership aims to support the long term improvement and regeneration of Dover and renew a sense of pride in our community.'

We will have to wait and see if that which is built turns out to be as architecturally impressive as the Hotel Burlington!

Market Square in 1897 and today. I don't suppose there are many people still in Dover that remember the trams. This is an early specimen, not yet sporting the decency boards on the upper deck. Dover Corporation Tramways opened in 1897 and lasted until 31 December 1936, when East Kent buses ran the next day. This one can be seen outside Killick & Back drapers and silk merchants and Binfields wine merchants.

The modern day view is hardly inspiring is it? 'Modern' angular blocks offering fried chicken, chocolate bars and school uniforms where there was once silk, kid-fitted corsets and Napoleon brandy!

Lucerne Terrace in 1909 and today. Lucerne Terrace is a row of late Victorian houses situated in Tower Hamlets between the Eagle public house and the railway bridge. This picture is on a postcard sent from Frank to his friend Gerty in 1909.

It reads, 'Received your welcome letter. Very many thanks. This is a photo of my mother and the house taken last year. My mother on right. Will write to you tomorrow without fail. Best of wishes and love, Frank'.

In 1909 the family living at this house were Riley or Reilly. In the 2009 photo one of the residents, Tony Cooper, is standing in the same place.

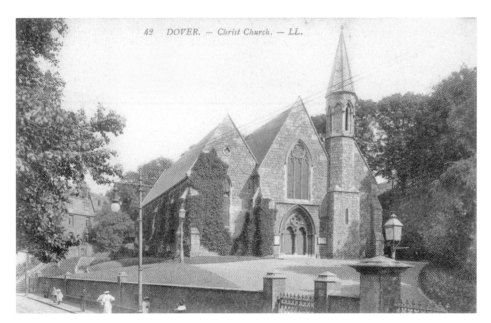

Christchurch, Folkestone Road *c.* 1930 and today. The site on which Christchurch
was built in 1844 was formerly military land belonging to the Board of Ordnance.
Considering its proximity to Western Heights this isn't at all surprising. Up the hill behind
the church is the North Military Road and across from that the Drop Redoubt fort.

The land was sold by the Board of Ordnance with a proviso that there would always
be space reserved in the congregation for fifty soldiers, plus officers.

The church was demolished in 1977 and the site was still vacant in 1988. I'm not
sure that the current flats are quite as impressive.

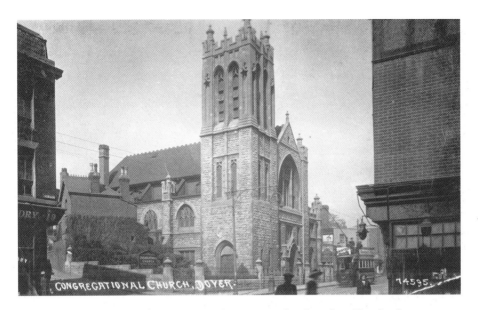

Congregational Church in the 1920s and in 2007. The church suffered a devastating fire on 22 September 2007, and is still a wreck at the time of writing, some two years later. In Bavington-Jones's book *Annals of Dover*, he states that due to consolidation of the Church:

> They have built a large and handsome church at the bottom of the High Street, a few places from the Maison Dieu. Its tower rises to a height of eighty feet, is a striking feature and the whole is an ornament to the Town. The cost of the building was between £9,000 and £10,000. The general style is gothic of the Lancastrian period. When this new church was opened on 7 September 1904 Zion Chapel, the original home of the Congregationalists was disposed of...

Let's hope they don't dispose of this building instead of rebuilding it.

This old picture of Dover taken from the castle dates from around 1875, and we can see that in the foreground the Shoulder of Mutton gun battery is nearing completion. If you look closely it is possible to see a pair of gun barrels lying in the road. Presumably these have yet to be mounted. The Hotel Burlington looks great from this angle, the photograph taken close to Dover Castle's Canon's Gate. Had the proposed 1870 Promenade Pier scheme got off the ground this view may have been quite different.

It is impossible to take the same view today due to the tree growth around Dover Castle which is mostly out of control, so the present image was taken from the roof of the keep. The gun battery is still there but hidden, rotting and routinely vandalised beneath the undergrowth. Of course the Hotel Burlington has been replaced by the Burlington House office block. This is progress, apparently.

Biggin Street in 1919 and today. I guess you could say that this view has hardly changed over the last century. The shops are still there, the church is still there and people are still busy going about their daily business. No motor cars in this early shot though – cars were only for the wealthy in those days.

Instead of Shoe Zone, Phones4U and the HSBC bank there was World Stores, Playfairs Bootmakers, Morris Bakers and George Mence Smith's 'Oil and Italian warehouse and household supply store'.

To the extreme left of the first photo you can make out the end of the Salem Chapel, mentioned elsewhere in this book (see page 63). Also check out the woman looking at the photographer at bottom left. She can be seen on other old photographic postcards of Dover. Perhaps she is the photographer's wife?

Castle and Castle Street, Dover.

Castle Street in around 1948 and today. The trams have only been gone for a little more than a decade in this late 1940s photograph. Igglesden and Graves' Dovorian restaurant is on the left and the well-known Flashmans on the right. Flashmans were renowned for their wide range of services including removals, funerals, storage, auctioneers and estate agents. The firm of Flashman & Co. evolved from the earlier business of George Flashman, who was listed as a cabinet-maker at various addresses in Dover as early as 1832.

Due to Hitler yet again, much of this area has been redeveloped in the decades after the Second World War. A Pricerite supermarket opened in the new building on the Flashman's site, which in turn became Courts furniture and carpets. Courts went into administration in 2007 and now the Heart Foundation sells white goods and furniture from there.

St James' Church pre-war and today. The history of old St James' is pretty well documented so we shan't dwell on it too much here. The church is assumed to be one of Dover's oldest churches and stands next door to what is probably Dover's oldest pub, the White Horse. Almost certainly referred to in the Domesday Book, it was originally a Saxon church, although the present ruin dates to the 1100s.

As well as a congregational meeting place the church was also used by the courts of the Barons of the Cinque Ports. The Victorians decided that St James' was too small and New St James' was built in 1860 in Maison Dieu Road, the old church being restored in 1869.

What we have left today is again a result of enemy action in the Second World War.

Biggin Street in the 1920s and today. The River
& District Cooperative Society was founded in
1879 by Radford Evans. By 1881 there were
965 consumer Co-op societies in Britain and
the River & District Co-op opened for business in
Dover town at Nos 14-16 Biggin Street in 1889,
opposite today's McDonald's restaurant.

The building above was built in 1921 (you can
see the date on the apex of the building) opposite
the Co-op's then existing shops. The Co-op left
Nos 14-16 Biggin Street in 1989 to open up a
much larger store at Charlton.

The once impressive Salem Chapel in Biggin Street disappeared in 1970 to make way for the new Boots store. The chapel was originally built in 1840, set back from the main street line in order to accommodate a small cemetery out front. But by 1880 the building had been enlarged and the cemetery removed. The main notice board outside the chapel dates this image to about 1904 when the chapel started fundraising in order to build a new Sunday school. The foundation stone was laid in 1909 in the space behind the chapel in the then premises of Harry Tolputt & Co. timber yard.

Following demolition of the chapel a new Baptist church was erected in Maison Dieu Road.

Although Castle Street is today's thoroughfare across town, the street only dates to 1897. Prior to this it was St James' Street that was the town's main east-west artery.

When this picture was taken in the 1930s the cinema hadn't been built, but there's still plenty of activity here. Can you see the poster on the wall of Stembrook Cottage advertising Teddy Baldock's boxing match? He was British Bantamweight champion from 1927, and his chief sparring partner was Johnny Curley, British Featherweight champion, 1925–1927.

There's also East's corn, hay and straw merchants, and Leney, Fremlin and Flint's brewery offices on the right.

There are thirty-seven Grade Two listed properties in Castle Street today.

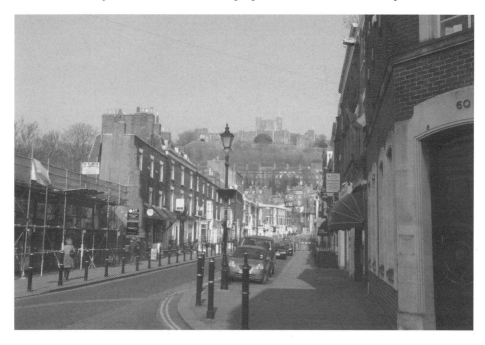

Maison Dieu House in the 1930s and today. The Maison Dieu was founded as a hospice in 1203 by Hubert de Burgh, Constable of Dover Castle and Earl of Kent. It was run by monks and its job was to give shelter to travellers and to look after the old and infirm.

During the Reformation the building was taken over by the Navy to use as a store and this lasted until 1834 when the Dover Corporation bought it with the intention of using it as a civic centre. A new jail (or gaol) was added in 1836, and the original building restored from about 1859 by architects Ambrose Poynter and William Burges. In 1881 the Connaught Hall was added.

Don't the hedges, trees and street lamps in the first image look nice? Another picture with no motor cars in it!

Dover College grounds in 1908 and in 2008. The Dover Pageant was first held in 1908 and was the idea of Louis Napoleon Parker, a popular playwright and musician. The idea was to portray Dover's cultural and historical story through narration, drama, music, dance and colourful period costumes.

The event's most recent Pageant Master is Mike McFarnell who restarted the pageant in 1983 and held it in Connaught Park. The most recent pageant to be organized by Mike was the 2008 event, marking its 100th anniversary. This is destined to be Dover's final pageant until someone new takes over the reigns.

Cannon Street in 1911 and today. The tram lines have gone and the dirt road has been replaced by block paving, but St Mary's Church provides an anchor to the past even though its adjacent shops have been replaced by Holland & Barrett, John Angel jewellers and Clinton Cards. Dorothy Perkins is also there occupying the once-new Tesco supermarket building. But activity in Biggin Street hasn't changed all that much over the last century. The locals still meet for coffee, go to church and shop in this familiar part of town!

Queen Elizabeth, the Queen Mother, in the Market Square in 1978 and a similar view today. In 1978 the Queen Mother was appointed Lord Warden and Admiral of the Cinque Ports and Constable of Dover Castle. Here she is in one of the state coaches slowly going past Dennis Weaver the stationer's with the Trustees Savings Bank in the background. Today the stationer's shop is the Dickens Corner café and the TSB has recently undergone refurbishment as the new joint local council and Kent County Council's 'Dover Gateway'. 'The Gateway is a customer-focused service offering residents convenient physical access to frontline customer advisors from a wide range of public services, in a modern retail setting.'

The Priory Hotel in 1960 and today. Fremlin the brewer was taken over by Whitbread in 1967 and the fascia of the Priory Hotel is advertising 'Kent's Best' next to the Fremlin's elephant logo.

The Priory Hotel was opened around 1877 and provided very convenient room and board, not to mention a pint or two for those alighting a train at the Priory Station opposite. There was also a Priory Tavern before 1877, but its exact location remains unknown.

The pub stood empty between 1988 and 1991 while the building was being renovated prior to re-opening by new landlords.

Market Square in the early 1900s and today. This busy street scene gives us a window to the past when it was possible to ride a tram through the town. There is so much going on in this picture and there are many businesses there which must have been household names when our grandparents and great-grandparents were around.

Just looking round the Market Square we can see Killick and Back the draper, Binfield Brothers wine merchants and Hogben & Son, corn, fodder and seed merchant.

Today's scene is almost unrecognisable as only a handful of the old buildings remain. Hopefully the Burlington House office block eyesore will soon be gone!

Folkestone Road in about 1910 and today. The most obvious thing about these pictures is how little it has changed. The tram lines have gone and there are cars now, but essentially the two views are the same.

The Engineer pub on the corner of Malvern Road is being converted into four flats and a detached house is being built to its rear as we write this. But this building started life as Laburnum Cottage and was converted to a pub in 1871 so there's a nice continuity about this.

Notable in the later picture are the gaps between the houses on the left, presumably the result of bomb damage. At least you can still post a letter at this point in Folkestone Road as you could when this old photo was taken!

Whitfield Avenue in 1905 and today. This is a great photograph which shows part of the London Regiment, TA, 4th Middlesex (Kensington) VRC Dover, presumably marching up the hill to Old Park Barracks. The regiment was disbanded in 1938 to become the 13th (County of London) Battalion, LR (Kensington). The scene looks particularly rural, the only buildings in view being some long-gone cottages, Buckland Paper Mill and the old tram shed. The tram shed was built in 1897, and of course we all know it now as the premises of Hollis Motors, the SEAT car dealer.

A lot has changed – the road has been tarmacked and the hill is now lined with late Edwardian terraced houses. The paper mill site is now empty and awaiting redevelopment. We will have to see what happens when this recession is over.

Castlemount School in about 1920 and today. Information about Castlemount is very sketchy. The building dates back to 1879 when it was run by Robert Chignall as a high class prep school. In 1911 it was taken over by French monks but soon commandeered by the War Office during the First World War to be used as barracking.

After the war the monks returned but the building was soon to become a school. Unfortunately this fantastic looking building was destroyed by arson in 1973. Today it's a housing estate and another impressive bit of Dover has gone for good.

Victoria Crescent around 1900 and today. This old photo taken from the Western Heights gives us an excellent view of the pre-war town and of the castle. Castle Street is evident on the left as St James' Street muddles its way across town from St James' Church which just manages to pop its head up above the houses on the right of the photo.

Victoria Crescent looks wonderful and the eye is immediately drawn to it. These mid-Victorian five-storey houses are mostly bedsits and flats now, but must once have been glorious family houses.

What is also evident are a few late Victorian buildings within the castle's curtain wall – most of which have since been demolished.

5

SEAFRONT

The latest change to Dover seafront is the building of a new sea sports centre at the western-most end of the front, not far from the old Hoverport site. The new centre that is nearing completion is an impressive structure in a continually changing setting.

The seafront has seen constant change over the centuries as the above picture illustrates. The Promenade Pier and the fishing boats have been and gone. Bomb damage, barbed wire entanglements from two world wars, Victorian and earlier gun batteries have all changed this popular part of Dover. Indeed, if it were not for change and the management of shingle drift along the front, the beach wouldn't be here at all.

The soon to be enlarged Western Docks will provide even more change as a new marina will be built next to Prince of Wales Pier, a new chapter in the story of Dover.

A general seafront view in about 1880 and today. Waterloo Crescent was built between 1834 and 1838 and was designed by Philip Hardwick, an important architect from this period who became architect and surveyor to the hospitals of Bridewell, Bethlehem, and to St Bartholomew's. He was also architect to the Greenwich Hospital, and did work at the Duke of Wellington's house in Hyde Park Corner.

In this early picture we can see Connaught House on the left, which became the Customs House and then turned into Dover Harbour Board offices. Waterloo Crescent was designed as three sections, the centre one containing nine houses, and the outside ones five houses each. The next terrace along is now the Churchill Hotel and the next, the Royal Cinque Ports Yacht Club.

The Gateway flats now replace the other large houses on the seafront and the Grand Hotel which were all lost during the war. Note the military hospital in the early picture which has disappeared from the modern view just next to Admiralty Lookout.

Guilford Battery in the early 1860s and today. Guilford Battery, one of Dover's coast defence batteries, has virtually vanished today. The site has been continuously altered to be home to a roller skating rink (1910), an open air cinema, a First World War RNAS seaplane station, and most recently, an Army recruitment centre. There was also an anti-aircraft battery near to these buildings during the Second World War. The site is currently privately owned but sadly derelict. Most of the land associated with the site's past has been absorbed and redeveloped into the A20 dual carriageway. If the aircraft hangers were still there today, they would stretch across the road and onto the promenade.

County Rink *c.* 1910 and today. As you drive down Jubilee Way and into Dover today you would pass over the site of the County Skating Rink. It jutted out from below the White Cliffs almost to the beach.

It was built in 1910 by Dover & District Rink Ltd and was intended to detract would-be skaters away from the Promenade Pier's rink. The attraction was built on part of the obsolete Guilford Battery next to Moat's Bulwark. It was opened by former mayor Sir William Crundall in August 1910, and well-known names in skating circles came to Dover including 'fancy and trick skating by Syd Martin' as well as Merry Martha, the champion female skater. In the same year the country's first open air cinema opened next door.

The rink didn't last long due to the building being converted into a seaplane hanger for the Royal Naval Air Service at the outbreak of the First World War.

Promenade Pier Regatta Day *c.* 1910 and today. The first Promenade Pier scheme arose in the 1870s but was refused by planners on the grounds that such a structure would spoil the bathing in Dover Bay. The 1891 scheme however did get off John Webster's drawing board and was opened in May 1893 by Lady Dickeson, wife of the mayor. A major repair was made necessary in 1895 when a storm managed to destroy a large section of the pier superstructure. The pier gained a pavilion in 1901 and this included reading rooms, a library and dance hall. The pier was a popular venue for afternoon and evening concerts in the summer months and roller skating was an added attraction when Herr Muller's Pomeranian Orchestra wasn't playing there. The body of Nurse Edith Cavell, the British nurse executed as a spy in 1915 by the Germans, was brought back to England via the Promenade Pier. She is buried in the grounds of Norwich Cathedral.

Unfortunately the pier company was not a commercial success and the structure was sold to the Admiralty in 1913 for £8,000, some £22,000 less than its total build cost. The pier was finally demolished in 1927 and most of its fixtures and fittings sold off at auction.

The Promenade in about 1920 and 2006. This is a simply wonderful view showing Dover's townsfolk relaxing on the seafront, just as they do today. There's even a bandstand in the background, and parasols aplenty. Plenty of people are taking advantage of the weather and spending their time on the beach – the Edwardian bathing machines are a thing of the past! The 2006 scene isn't that much different really, is it? The comparable image is of Dover Regatta with hundreds of people enjoying themselves with friends and family at this summer event.

Granville Gardens in September 1933 and today. Granville Gardens were laid out during 1878 by the Dover Harbour Board on the site of the old seafront baths. The gardens were a popular venue to go and listen to music in the summer months. The Dover Corporation Band gave regular afternoon and evening concerts throughout the summer season until the outbreak of war. The Corporation Band could be a different band each season, but there was always competition between it and the bands that played on the Promenade Pier.

To quote the Dover Musical Record from 16 December 1901, 'The Corporation Band gave some excellent programmes in Granville Gardens... to large audiences, though not so large as last year, owing to the attractions on the Promenade Pier.' Mr James Fairbairn's band was the Corporation Band for that and the previous seasons.

There was also roller skating at Granville Gardens and this, together with the Dover Rink round the corner and the gardens' musical endeavours, helped to plunge the Promenade Pier Company into financial ruin.

The India Monument in the early 1960s and today. The India or Rifles Monument was unveiled in 1861 to commemorate the fallen of the 1st Battalion of 60th Royal Rifles during the Indian campaigns of 1857, 1858 and 1859. Behind it are the remains of Camden Crescent and the Dover Stage hotel, built in the 1957 by Barwick and demolished in 1988.

Today's scene is minus the Dover Stage but plus Burlington House. I'm not sure which is worse!

6

ENVIRONS

So far we've focused on the town of Dover but there are some equally interesting sites, buildings and landscapes in the outlying countryside. In this short section we'll take a look at a few of them, and to start off with, the above picture shows a sports day at Burgoyne Heights. Unfortunately this picture was undated but looks like the 1920s from the cloche hats, etc. What is especially nice about this one is the smartly dressed lady and the table of trophies and prizes, and the photographer taking her picture!

Langdon Prison in around 1920 and today. Langdon Prison once stood on the site of the present 'National Trust Saga Gateway' to the White Cliffs of Dover, to give it its rightful name. It was built in 1884/85 to house convict labourers that were to build a harbour scheme that never materialised. The prison closed in 1896 but re-opened in 1901 as a military prison. This was subsequently closed seven years later but again re-opened, this time as a troop transit station during the First World War.

Following the war, the site was partially demolished and was largely cleared by 1925. What was left was used during the Second World War but the establishment was finally shut in 1948 and pretty well everything else demolished.

The National Trust took over the site in 1988 and the new Saga visitor centre was opened by the conservationist David Bellamy in May 1999

Broadlees Bottom about 1930 and today. Can you remember when we last had a decent snowfall like this? Everyone, young and old, is enjoying sledging down the Northfall Meadow recreation ground in this 1930s scene. Those that aren't taking part are enjoying watching the daring sledgers. This area has undergone many changes of use over time. The Victorians built a rifle range here, there was a twentieth-century military hutted camp on the site, together with an obstacle course, a golf course and nearby motor transport sheds and a sergeants' mess.

The two nineteenth-century earthworks in the background, Hudson's and Horseshoe Bastions, from left to right, are still there and much overgrown. These were designed by Brigadier Twiss and were constructed around the same time that the castle's mural towers were reduced in height.

The MT (motor transport) sheds were pulled down and the sergeants' mess suffered from arson about a decade ago. Bleriot landed near here, but the change that has most impacted this corner of Dover is of course, the road. The A2 cuts through here on its way to the Jubilee Way flyover.

Aycliffe Cottages in the 1920s and 2006. When Nos 1-8 Aycliffe Cottages were built, those responsible could hardly have envisaged the rest of the Aycliffe estate. These houses have changed very little since being built but the area around them has been transformed. Lying in the shadow of Shakespeare's Cliff behind a concrete fence, the A20 dual carriageway cuts them off from the cliff edge.

As a backdrop Western Heights is always there, but the King Lear pub has now been demolished.

1832. Traversée de la Manche – Endroit par où est passé Blériot avant d'atterrir à Douvres. L.V. & Cⁱᵉ

Langdon Cliffs in 1909 and today. 2009 is a special year for Dover as it celebrates the 100th anniversary of the crossing of the English Channel by aeroplane by Louis Bleriot in 1909. Of course, he landed in the Northfall Meadow behind Dover Castle having covered twenty-seven miles in thirty-seven minutes and landed on 25 July 1909. Big celebrations were held around the town this summer to commemorate the occasion.

This snowy 2009 image has a lot more trees in it than it once did and much of this has been cleared in order to provide some trails around Bleriot's Memorial and to make the site more accessible. The coast guard cottages are still evident, and I shan't even mention the harbour!

Blériot Memorial, Dover. The inscription reads:-
"After making the first Channel Flight by Aeroplane,"
Louis Blériot landed at this spot on Sunday 25th July, 1909.

The Langdon Cliffs in 1909 and today. The 2009 image has a lot more trees than the earlier photograph, although much of this has now been cleared in order to provide some trails around Bleriot's memorial and to make the site more accessible. There is a stone tablet in front of Bleriot's granite 'aeroplane' which reads: 'After making the first Channel flight by aeroplane Lois Bleriot landed at this spot on Sunday 25th July 1909. This memorial was presented by the Aero Club of the United Kingdom by Alexander Duckham.'

Aycliffe Camp around 1900 and today. This simply wonderful photograph shows the area we know today as Aycliffe and the A20 dual carriageway, but infinitely more interesting. This is a military camp of course, and this sort of thing was a familiar sight around Dover, particularly when there was a military review at hand.

These reviews would, broadly speaking, be a mock battle when troops would arrive and all the batteries along this part of the coast would fire upon our own ships at sea. These must have presented a fantastic spectacle to the people and press of Dover.

There is a good chunk of Western Heights in this old picture, some of which is still extant, although hidden by trees now. The tented camp is formally laid out and if you look closely there are sheep grazing nearby and some field guns in the centre of the picture by the road.

If those men could travel a hundred years into the future they would think they were in a different place.

Sunny Corner in the 1920s. In his 1980 book, *Sunny Corner, England*, Ray Langabeer wrote about the plans to demolish his house which was built by his grandfather in about 1875 in order to build the A20 extension road.

Sergeant-Major John Langabeer bought the plot of land, now where the A20 'Megger' roundabout is on his retirement from the army. He had been stationed in the nearby Archcliffe Fort with the Royal Engineers during his military service.

After much consultation and after examining other routes, such as tunnelling a road under Western Heights, the new road smashed through Sunny Corner in the early 1990s. Not only did the scheme mean ploughing through Sunny Corner, but also destroying the Barrier Ditch, one of the moats at Western Heights, the Second World War anti-invasion flame barrage apparatus in that ditch and the South Lines Battery, a Victorian gun battery on the cliff edge. It also meant the removal of part of the front of Archcliffe Fort, which is now lapped by the new dual-carriageway.

7

DOVER AT WAR

This small section documents the town during the last few days of the Second World War through the lens of the US Army Press Department. A reporter and photographer were here in May 1945 and their photos show a torn and battered town. To the best of our knowledge, these five pictures have not been published since 1945.

Athol Terrace 1945 and today. The three boys in the photo are, from left to right: Colin Gibbs who lived at No. 15 Athol Terrace, Leslie Day from No. 41 East Cliff and Michael Culley, also from Dover. The lads showed the press officer round the Esplanade tunnels, those that run from what is now the swimming pool site all the way through the cliffs to Athol. The tunnel was then being used as an air raid shelter.

The tunnels are reputed to be named Esplanade in reference to the set of tunnels within Dover Castle, some of which are now marketed as the Secret Wartime Tunnels. That is, A, B, C, D and E – Annex, Bastion, Casemate, DUMPY and Esplanade.

For those car fans among us, this Second World War Jeep was one of over 640,000 units built by Willys and Ford between 1941 and 1945 for the US Army and her Allies. The modern version seen here is the Jeep Wrangler, made by the Chrysler Corporation, which once had its UK headquarters in Dover.

Hotel Burlington in 1945 and today. This once proud building suffered badly at the hands of Hitler's cross-channel artillery, and the building was eventually demolished in 1949 as it was considered to be unsafe. Prior to this the Italianate tower to the east of the main building was blown up in September 1941 by the 171 Tunnelling Company, Royal Engineers; again as it was considered to be in a dangerous state.

The tanks are parked up in the once picturesque Clarence Lawn, which was a pleasure garden between the Burlington and the Promenade Pier, which had been demolished some eighteen years previously. All the tanks are American Sherman derivatives, mainly Fireflies.

Dover Promenade in 1945 and 2008. This, another of the photographs taken by the US Army, shows amphibious vehicles, LVT (A) 2s to be precise, on the promenade opposite long-demolished terraces. Outside the terraces is a line of four army low-loaders, perhaps to take the amphibious vehicles away. The terraces were demolished after the war due to their extensive damage. This spot is now the Gateway Flats. In the distance is the old Dover Rink building.

In 2008 a cycle race was organised by 'Help for Heroes', a fundraising charity for wounded servicemen. It ran from Portsmouth to Caen in France and back to London. The cyclists crossed the Channel in HMS *Bulwark*, being loaded and unloaded each side of the Channel by the Royal Navy landing craft we see here. There were four of these craft, each carrying seventy cyclists. The event raised about £1 million for the charity.

Woolcomber Street in 1945 and 2003. This is the final picture here taken by the US Army. It shows a very battered seafront area. The Hotel Burlington is distinct and still impressive in its knocked-about state. As mentioned elsewhere here, the main Italianate tower has long been reduced to rubble for safety reasons. What is alarming is that there is smoke coming out of one of the chimneys on the left. It can't have been very safe or very comfortable living.

This 2003 photo taken from the top of the Burlington House office block shows the same area from the opposite direction. It doesn't look like it's changed much since the initial post-war clearance was carried out. Hopefully the promised redevelopment soon to be carried out will give the area a new found pride.

Other titles published by The History Press

Haunted Dover
LORRAINE SENCICLE

Featuring tales from the seventeenth century to the present day, this exhaustive A–Z guide reveals the mysterious side of historic Dover. Situated at the narrowest part of the English Channel, Dover has had its fair share of waifs and strays travelling through it over the course of many years. As well as retelling these chilling tales, Sencicle delves into the history surrounding the stories to discover the probable reasons behind the hauntings. This spine-tingling book will fascinate anyone who dares to read it.

978 0 7524 4859 6

Murder & Crime Dover
JANET CAMERON

Those who fell foul of the law in Kent faced a horrible fate: some were thrown to their deaths from the top of Dover's iconic white cliffs, whilst others were hanged, quartered, burnt or buried alive. Yet still the criminal fraternity of Kent went undeterred. This fascinating book contains tales of thwarted rivals and wicked soldiers, desperate mothers, licentious monks and disreputable women. With more than fifty illustrations, this chilling catalogue of murderous misdeeds is bound to captivate anyone interested in the criminal history of the area.

978 0 7524 3978 5

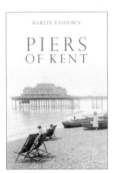

Piers of Kent
MARTIN EASDOWN

With its long coastline and mild climate, the county of Kent was at the forefront of the growth of the British seaside resort. From the 1860s, a 'mania' developed amongst resorts to erect a showpiece pleasure pier, with Margate, in Kent, having its first pier in 1855. Today, only Gravesend's Town and Royal Terrace, Deal's post-war concrete pier and a stub of Herne Bay survive.

978 0 7524 4220 4

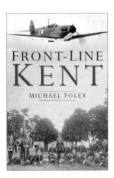

Front-Line Kent
MICHAEL FOLEY

Kent has always been on England's first line of defence. Many people in the county have lived closer to the enemy in Europe than they did to London. This book delves into the long history of military Kent, from Roman forts to Martello towers, from the ambitious Royal Military Canal to wartime airfields and underground Cold War installations.

978 0 7509 4460 1

Visit our website and discover thousands of other History Press books.

www.thehistorypress.co.uk

The History Press